KWJCE
11/05

D1032901

I USE MATH/USO LAS MATEMÁTICAS

I USE MATH AT THE GAME/
USO LAS MATEMÁTICAS EN EL JUEGO DE PELOTA

Joanne Mattern

Reading consultant/Consultora de lectura: Susan Nations, M.Ed., author/literacy coach/consultant

Please visit our web site at: www.earlyliteracy.cc
For a free color catalog describing Weekly Reader® Early Learning Library's list
of high-quality books, call 1-877-445-5824 (USA) or 1-800-387-3178 (Canada).
Weekly Reader® Early Learning Library's fax: (414) 336-0164.

Library of Congress Cataloging-in-Publication Data available upon request from publisher.
Fax (414) 336-0157 for the attention of the Publishing Records Department.

ISBN 0-8368-6000-4 (lib. bdg.)
ISBN 0-8368-6007-1 (softcover)

This edition first published in 2006 by
Weekly Reader® Early Learning Library
A Member of the WRC Media Family of Companies
330 West Olive Street, Suite 100
Milwaukee, WI 53212 USA

Copyright © 2006 by Weekly Reader® Early Learning Library

Managing editor: Valerie J. Weber
Art direction: Tammy West
Cover design and page layout: Dave Kowalski
Photo research: Diane Laska-Swanke
Photographer: Gregg Andersen
Translators: Tatiana Acosta and Guillermo Gutiérrez

Printed in the United States of America

1 2 3 4 5 6 7 8 9 09 08 07 06 05

Note to Educators and Parents

Reading is such an exciting adventure for young children! They are beginning to integrate their oral language skills with written language. To encourage children along the path to early literacy, books must be colorful, engaging, and interesting; they should invite the young reader to explore both the print and the pictures.

I Use Math is a new series designed to help children read about using math in their everyday lives. In each book, young readers will explore a different activity and solve math problems along the way.

Each book is specially designed to support the young reader in the reading process. The familiar topics are appealing to young children and invite them to read and reread again and again. The full-color photographs and enhanced text further support the student during the reading process.

In addition to serving as wonderful picture books in schools, libraries, homes, and other places where children learn to love reading, these books are specifically intended to be read within an instructional guided reading group. This small group setting allows beginning readers to work with a fluent adult model as they make meaning from the text. After children develop fluency with the text and content, the book can be read independently. Children and adults alike will find these books supportive, engaging, and fun!

Nota para los maestros y los padres

¡Leer es una aventura tan emocionante para los niños pequeños! A esta edad están comenzando a integrar su manejo del lenguaje oral con el lenguaje escrito. Para animar a los niños en el camino de la lectura incipiente, los libros deben ser coloridos, estimulantes e interesantes; deben invitar a los jóvenes lectores a explorar la letra impresa y las ilustraciones.

Uso las matemáticas es una nueva colección diseñada para que los niños lean textos sobre el uso de las matemáticas en su vida diaria. En cada libro, los jóvenes lectores explorarán una actividad diferente y resolverán problemas de matemáticas. Cada libro está especialmente diseñado para ayudar a los jóvenes lectores en el proceso de lectura. Los temas familiares llaman la atención de los niños y los invitan a leer y releer una y otra vez. Las fotografías a todo color y el tamaño de la letra ayudan aún más al estudiante en el proceso de lectura.

Además de servir como maravillosos libros ilustrados en escuelas, bibliotecas, hogares y otros lugares donde los niños aprenden a amar la lectura, estos libros han sido especialmente concebidos para ser leídos en un grupo de lectura guiada. Este contexto permite que los lectores incipientes trabajen con un adulto que domina la lectura mientras van determinando el significado del texto. Una vez que los niños dominan el texto y el contenido, el libro puede ser leído de manera independiente. ¡Estos libros les resultarán útiles, estimulantes y divertidos a niños y a adultos por igual!

— Susan Nations, M.Ed., author, literacy coach,
and consultant in literacy development

I am going to my first baseball game with Dad, my sister, and my brother. These are great seats! We are sitting close to the field.

- - - - - - - - - - - - - - - -

Voy a mi primer partido de béisbol con mi papá, mi hermana y mi hermano. ¡Estos puestos son fantásticos! Estamos sentados cerca del campo.

How many of us are there?

¿Cuántas personas de mi familia vinimos al partido?

5

There are players from each team on the field. The coaches and umpires are on the field, too.

En el campo hay jugadores de los dos equipos. Los entrenadores y los árbitros también están en el campo.

How many people on the baseball field are wearing red shirts?

¿Cuántos jugadores con camiseta roja hay en el campo?

There are nine innings in most baseball games. The scoreboard shows the score in each inning.

En la mayoría de los partidos de béisbol se juegan nueve entradas. Los marcadores muestran la puntuación en cada entrada.

After four innings, how many innings will be left to play?

Después de cuatro entradas, ¿cuántas entradas faltan por jugar?

AT BAT	BALL	STRIKE	OUT	H/E

		1	2	3	4	5	6	7	8	9		RUNS	HITS	ERRORS
GUEST														
TWINS														

ANIMATED DISPLAYS

9

The batter's job is to hit the ball. If he swings and misses the ball three times, he is out.

- - - - - - - - - - - - - - - -

El bateador tiene que golpear la pelota. Si intenta batear y falla tres veces, está eliminado o out.

This batter has swung twice and missed.
How many more swings does he get before he is out?

Este bateador ha fallado dos intentos. ¿Cuántas veces
más puede batear antes de quedar eliminado?

11

The scoreboard shows how many runs each team scores. It also shows what inning it is.

— — — — — — — — — — — — —

El marcador muestra cuántas carreras, o runs, anota cada equipo. También muestra en qué entrada está el partido.

How many runs have the Twins scored so far?

¿Cuántas carreras han anotado los Twins hasta el momento?

AT BAT BALL STRIKE OUT H/E

	1	2	3	4	5	6	7	8	9	RUNS	HITS	ERRORS
GUEST												
TWINS												

MIKE
REDMOND

ANIMATED DISPLAYS

13

I am so thirsty. My dad gave me ten dollars to buy a cold drink. The cold drink cost three dollars.

Tengo mucha sed. Mi papá me dio diez dólares para que compre un refresco. El refresco cuesta tres dólares.

How much change will I get back?

¿Cuánto cambio me devolverán?

Now the other team has scored some runs. The game is tied.

Ahora el otro equipo ha anotado algunas carreras. Hay un empate.

How many runs has the guest team scored?

¿Cuántas carreras ha anotado el otro equipo?

16

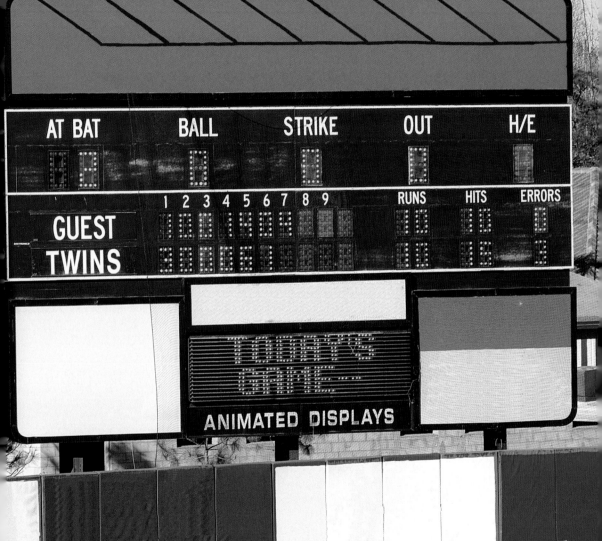

AT BAT   BALL   STRIKE   OUT   H/E

1 2 3 4 5 6 7 8 9   RUNS   HITS   ERRORS

GUEST

TWINS

TODAY'S
GAME

ANIMATED DISPLAYS

17

Each inning has two halves. After the first half of the seventh inning, everyone stands up to stretch. I like to stretch and sing along with the songs.

- - - - - - - - - - - - - - - - -

Cada entrada tiene dos mitades. Después de la primera mitad de la séptima entrada, todos nos paramos para estirarnos. Me gusta estirarme y cantar con los demás.

One half of the seventh inning is over.
How many halves are left in this inning?

Una mitad de la séptima entrada ya se ha acabado.
¿Cuántas mitades de esta entrada faltan por jugar?

We got out of the game at 3:00. It will take us a half hour to get home.

- - - - - - - - - - - - - - - - -

Salimos del juego a las 3:00. Nos tomará media hora llegar a casa.

What time will we get home?

¿A qué hora llegaremos a casa?

Glossary

coaches — people who train players

innings — parts of a baseball game

runs — a score in baseball

scored — made a point in a game

strike — to swing and miss the ball

team — a group of people who play together

tied — when two teams have the same score

umpire — a person who makes sure the game is played fairly

Glosario

anotar — marcar un punto en el juego

árbitro — persona que se asegura de que no haya trampas en el juego

carreras — puntos en el béisbol

empate — cuando los dos equipos tienen los mismos puntos en un juego

entradas — partes de un juego de béisbol

entrenadores — personas que preparan a los jugadores

equipo — grupo de personas que juegan juntas

strike — intento de bateo fallido

Answers

Page 4 – 4
Page 6 – 9
Page 8 – 5
Page 10 – 1
Page 12 – 10
Page 14 – $7
Page 16 – 10
Page 18 – 1
Page 20 – 3:30

Respuestas

Página 4 – 4
Página 6 – 9
Página 8 – 5
Página 10 – 1
Página 12 – 10
Página 14 – $7
Página 16 – 10
Página 18 – 1
Página 20 – 3:30

For More Information/Más información

Books

Baseball. Cynthia Fitterer Klingel
  (Child's World)
Counting: Follow That Fish! Math Monsters (series).
  John Burnstein (Weekly Reader® Early
  Learning Library)

Libros

Béisbol en los barrios/Baseball in the Barrios.
  Henry Horenstein (Sagebrush)

Soy buena para las matemáticas. Eileen M. Day
  (Heinemann Library)

Websites

Math Baseball

www.funbrain.com/math
Answer math problems to score runs in this online
baseball learning game.

Index

Índice

About the Author

Joanne Mattern is the author of more than 130 books for children. Her favorite subjects are animals, history, sports, and biography. Joanne lives in New York State with her husband, three young daughters, and three crazy cats.

Información sobre la autora

Joanne Mattern ha escrito más de 130 libros para niños. Sus temas favoritos son los animales, la historia, los deportes y las biografías. Joanne vive en el estado de Nueva York con su esposo, sus tres hijas pequeñas y tres gatos juguetones.